Unmaking Atoms

Magdalena Ball

Unmaking Atoms

Unmaking Atoms
ISBN 978 1 76041 282 1
Copyright © text Magdalena Ball 2017
Cover image: Hand Floating Atoms © Ezume Images

First published 2017 by
Ginninderra Press
PO Box 3461 Port Adelaide 5015 Australia
www.ginninderrapress.com.au

Contents

Artefacts	9
The Last Report of the Day	11
Charitable Crumb	13
Luminous Air	15
Artefacts	16
Right Angles to Reality	18
Atomic Mess	20
Past Life	22
Catalyst	24
Ashes for the Earth	26
Yellow Jacquard	28
Salting the Wound	31
Orthonym	33
Beginner's Mind	35
Salting the Wound	37
Almost	39
Rough Ride	41
Years Ago	43
Static	45
Trojan Horse	46
Landscape at Pentecost	48
Irrational Heart	49
Most of Everything is Nothing	57
The No Times Times	59
Encroachment Spells Erosion	60
Walking Into Eternity	62
Life Dreaming	63
Radiology	65
Maven on Mars	66

In the Frame	68
Shallots and Garlic	70
Silence; the coffee cup, the table	71
Echo Chamber	72
Most of Everything is Nothing	74
Six Realms	75

Robin's Eye	**77**
Brown Quail (*Coturnix ypsilophora*)	79
Coral Composition	81
Alien World	83
Roseanna	85
Reflecting sphere	88
The Happiness Project	89
Ascetic Stitch	91
Cruel Fortune	93
Robin's Eye	95
Mirror Neurons	97
Old Wounds	99
Circus Factory	100
Mobius Strip	101
Television, the sea, the window	102
Cold Mirror	103
Harnessing Wind	104
Migration	105
Decoherence Through the Window	106
Inanimate	107
Dark Matter Wants to be Alone	108
Angel	110

A Cloud Withdrew	**111**
Mapping Pluto	113
Absences	115

Stargazy	117
Mourner's Kaddish	118
Unmaking Atoms	120
A Cloud Withdrew	122
Venus in the East Before Sunrise	123
Portfolio	125
Weather Situations	126
Pranayama	128
Inside Your Darkest Everything	129

Hieroglyphics — 135

Autotopography	137
Dhurbar Square	139
Energy Conservation	141
Hieroglyphics	142
Unchanging unceasing murmur	146
Nature's Observatory	148
Woman with her hair loose	151
Entopic Imagery	153
Probability Waves	155
Essential Whites	156
In Situ	157
Gargantua redacted	158

Velocity or Pause — 159

RNA World	161
Velocity or Pauses	164
Misinformation Effect	166
Redhead Beach	168
Winter Apples	170
Watagan Walk	171
Free Radicals	173
Dogstar	175

Lacuna	176
Image of the day	178
Planet Nine	179
Fractals of Fractals	181
Qualia	182
Solar Collections	184
Out of the Blue	185
Intelligent Equations	187
Notes	188
Acknowledgements	189

Artefacts

The Last Report of the Day

I saw you, Adrienne Rich.
In my dream we were
walking like old friends
conspicuously cool
our maps drawn
before we took up pens
eyes searching for something
deeper than the wrinkles on our skin.

I felt your hand, crooked with arthritis
brush mine
in the depths of my consciousness
like a stirring of memory
you became every mother
I had ever lost
to a bigger cause
the world too hungry
the lines too sharp
for me to cross.

I was a little girl then
all my unspoken need
pulsing like a lighthouse
your untranslatable language
transmitted through my pores
a scent you recognised.

You didn't need to say anything
the *battery of signals*
that battered you
like we've all been battered
I felt those signals in my shoulders
hunched against a rising wind.

Gently, but with reasonable force
you pushed my scapulae back
told me, sternly
like any mother would
to stand up straight.

Charitable Crumb

'The sun set in the same sea; the same odd sun / rose from the sea' –
Elizabeth Bishop, 'Crusoe in England'

It is still dark
the river ripples
below us
while we drink coffee
on that balcony
together at last
after so many years
of entanglement
remote whispers
down the phone line
and later
whatever means
we could find to keep
the conversation
going.

Now you lean in close
like a confidante
talk about observation
and longing
all that you never had
mother, father, siblings, lovers
the loss that kept coming
like water
suspended over blue-grey stones.

In the hard mouth of the world
we find sudden softness
released into our fingers
that intertwine and separate
typing words breathlessly
against the rising steam of time
our mutual loss holding us here
with this bottomless cup
and the same odd sun.

Luminous Air

'Come and see my shining palace built upon the sand!' – Edna St Vincent Millay, 'A Few Figs from Thistles'

We forgot the secret again
lost on the island
you in your bare beauty
bringing up goosebumps
in the audience
while you tilted your head
whispering small, small.

The rain was full of ghosts
that night
the air luminous
with immortality.

When I next caught your eye
it was already too late
your heart broke over memory's halls
marbled fingers tapping
against my breath
like dried figs in the early hour.

I crawled through indiscriminate dust
looking for the missing light.

Despite the smooth departure
you were not resigned
not found in easy places
even by the silver knocking
of silent fingers
where death becomes being.

Artefacts

This pile of rubble
buried with my body
fire-cracked
left to moulder.

Fumbling through
the detritus
that holds you here
strange attractor
forms a recurring pattern
out of chaos.

All these things slipped
from my home
bought, displayed, worn
against the skin
the beating of a heart
a memory of scent
powdered into ever finer
recursive detail
a Mandelbrot of loss.

Broken artefacts and bottles
scattered beads
excavated
as broken promises
repeating fractals
material culture
can't bring back my face
though you keep looking.

Remnants along the filaments
parataxis of chipped glass
objectifying time
not bringing
me back.

Right Angles to Reality

On the bridge of time
I waited in a dream
toes curled along the edge
lips pulled back in expectation.

It could have been anywhere
scanning radio frequencies
cold and bright
as if this alien moon were *the moon*.

Enceladus spouting water
against a frozen heart
in need of heat.

Open strings
ultrasound
pressure waves
infrasound
an unheard symphony played
in the vacuum of space
while I waited
ninety degrees to the membrane
the middle of nowhere
nothing picking
up the signal.

In place of mourning I laughed
silently, hysterically
a synecdoche
for all those things
we pretended were real.

That big open mouth
the echoing void
your waving hand.

Atomic Mess

When your last
fractured breath came
condensation of
a lifetime, I wasn't ready
but you were

pulled in constricting circles
battened the hatches
bolted the door

I felt the cut at thirty thousand feet
watched the cord slacken
lost the sonic heartbeat
before I arrived

after that
there was more silence
than I knew existed

fearless, you slid
into the atomic mess
safe from a life that assaulted
you at every turn

in all this quiet
how will I hear that song
your breath exhaled into cold air
gypsy lullaby
on my lips

does inheritance
provide solace
now you're no longer
here reminding me
to be brave?

Past Life

There are no chains
to hold that fragile
body down
no locks you can't unpick.

Earth waves in and out
of your vision
just one world of many
exquisite
but not alone.

It took so many years
to find what you knew already
the gemstone
in your pocket.

Here you are
ready to try again
eyes full of stars
not myopic
cataract-ridden dreams.

Real hyper-giants
fusing hydrogen to helium
shining with nuclear energy
burning through billions of lives.

Where will you alight
what love
will unhinge you
this time
entering the flesh again.

How will I
with all my limitations
deep in samsara
crawling on broken knees
find you?

Is the connection between us
me in this life
you in another
so tenuous
untethered by those bonds
we once thought permanent?

Catalyst

My body expands
a balloon of skin
stretching

this is the catalyst
nails against the skin
breathe into it

all this bee stung beauty
thrown at me
without preamble
fracture my eyelids
there's no other way
but to ease in

once the chemical reaction starts
reagents glistening
there's no stopping it.

Trying to remain hard
I soften into change
coughing up
preconceptions
like lumps of history

no matter how hard
I try to forget
my body keeps reminding me
at the atomic level
I'm little more than
a substrate-attached, heat-driven
26-element molecule

subject to reactivity
and mathematical constructs.

Ashes for the Earth

Walking slowly
distraction of hearth left
to those that still bleed
a forest grows around me.

Lichen and stone
vine, rock and leaf
each footstep goes deeper
into the soil
breaking down the loam
beneath incorporeal feet
crushing barriers in my mind.

This forest is a city
the buildings of memory
tug and sting
phantom pain
whispered against this journey.

Sound comes in even pulses
breath is a dream I once had
in the days when trees were buildings
and fear was a girdle
maintaining form.

My body unravels
through this
nameless place
those attachments
the hunger of the living
can be shed
though not easily.

I still taste salt on my tongue
still hear the soft call
of my children
their fingers looking for me
in black and white lacunae
echoes in the disappearing air
even as I continue
making ashes for the earth

it's too late to turn back.

Yellow Jacquard

I've never liked yellow
in spite of the sun, daffodils,
lemons, bananas
yellow as adjective feels wan
like the jacquard sofa
inherited, with your earrings
cashmeres, jackets, silks.

It wouldn't fit in the suitcase.

Those old fashioned
inappropriately cheerful
periwinkles and dahlias
how do I even know what they're
called or the way we used to
laugh at all the colour you filled
the house with while I always
went for neutrals
though I was the bold one.

All this is to say

I guess you won't be insulted
if I look away from this unkind
gift I can't face because after all
that pain, running up and down the stairs
positive thinking and careful eating
you didn't get well and those stupidly
happy flowers continue to bloom on the sofa
you left behind with everything else
including the watch I bought you for your
last birthday, still ticking while your
own heart no longer does.

I don't want to sit on yellow flowers
even if it's what
you would have wanted.

I'd rather imagine
in some alternative universe
where you're taking note of
my transgressions
you're pursing your lips
and saying
in your sharpest *red* voice
'tsk, tsk.'

Salting the Wound

Orthonym

My mother moved from
one name to another
stripping off identity
rather than papering it on
each marriage a chance
to get this thing
called normal right.

Each failure a mess
cleaned away
to the apartment incinerator.

With so many shifts
I was never certain how
concrete my own name was
stereotyping me
as such a name might
Jew, white, American
or whether, by virtue of
subsuming my name into another
I had cowardly turned
on those identities.

The older I get
the further my name
recedes into roles, pseudonym, labels
papier mâché strips of newspaper
over a balloon core
drying and shrinking beneath
the plaster.

After all these years and layers
is it even feasible to consider
unwinding the strips
and trying to do better.

What if, after the painful
unravelling
I find the core shrivelled
years of compression
contracting that centre to nothing.

Would I forever be stuck
in namelessness; a nomad
looking for a home
lost in that lonely place
where skin meets bone.

Beginner's Mind

The end of a day
removed for one
intake of breath
from hullabaloo
finding flight in transition
from perception to conception
flying and falling in syncopated
beat like loss.

If I weren't here, sitting stock still
counting intake and outtake of breath
with each bony click
that says 'still alive'
but not quite living
I could be on my way somewhere
this even respiration turned ragged gasp
running, like Buddha himself
into glory, like you did
lips parted in ultimate freedom
leaving me with all this
responsibility
all this breath.

I know
I should be over this by now
nothing is permanent
but it always come back
the lure of grief
your curse of holiness
the no-self
I only saw as selfishness.

It's possible, even likely
that the selfishness was mine
that I never let you go
never learned,
despite all the drills
the mantras
the daily practice
the art of renunciation.

Salting the Wound

Behind the garden where no one goes any more
ice is melting.

Water flows slowly past rocks, lichen,
shards of things discarded.

It would be easy to catch something here:
a cold, a fish, your death.

I find your death among the shards
lift it to the air.
It's not as clean as I expected it to be.

The colours meld with my fingers
dirtying the nails, and then dissolve into my hands.

You were always afraid of germs.

I fall asleep, mouth open
to any passing bacteria that might chance
upon my lips, eyes flickering in REM
while the water rises.

A memory of moon settles
liquid and silvery into my skin.

Now I'm really with you
inside your death; your life
the flow of mercury that
doesn't distinguish between states.

You should never mix electricity with water
but here I am
exuding heat energy into a wavering stream.

The shock brings me back to life
opening my eyes into the pain of this moment

my pulsating body jammed against rocks, lichen
shards of things discarded.

Almost

your heartbeat
slows to seconds
a razor edge

between life and death
whispers against my skin
the knife cuts

breath turns icy whine
your ghost hovers
frequencies you courted

in braver days
when morning meant awakening
and future was real

the wind
the cold room
a fading light

we huddle
your body in state
present and absent

the chain of those
who pull
against us
feel the tug
pull back hard
into the pain

facing the fear
we're learning to love
the life you've left us
ever onwards almost

Rough Ride

On one of those nights
when rain falls hard
a gust of wind
slams the door
windows close
against the storm

I shut my eyes tightly
so it hurts a little
and imagine myself
cycling the long driveway

unhampered by beauty
sunshine or daylight
the road is rocky rough
skinny legs unaccustomed to pedalling
don't stop me

inside fires burn
the bed might be inviting
but I force
myself further
into the great chaos

broken down into
flying atoms
whirlwind planet x-treme
it's not what you'd call nice
right now
I don't need nice

slamming through gully-washers
water flying over the rims
a little dice with chance

carrying my weakness
like a backpack of garbage
wheels slide deep
into the atomic pool
wet, unruly, free
coming home to what I really am
under skin and bone
through these
fleshy hominid contractions.

Years Ago

Years ago
under silent observation
you pulled out a tear
silvery slick in the morning
inside was a memory
too harsh to set free
sealed in that lipid layer
forever captured against your cheek.

Beneath the sandpit
half the world rages
pulling hair from their teeth
driving haphazardly through
the insane rain of life.

I wanted you to be the other half
willed you into that role
closed one eye and saw you
serene.

Now I find you weren't the only one
half blind
my own serenity
hanging like
slaughtered beasts
to bleed.

Somewhere in there
water is flowing
the burning secret
let go
despite the fear
you hoarded in that tiny
unexpressed orb.

Static

this nightmare place
of wishes and whirlwinds
chaos flows
electrical charge
from my fingertips

sunrise dissipates sensation
to memory
fragment scraps
whatever we've held
narrated, captured on film
in blue light
photoshopped to nostalgia

here you are in static
the ghost I cling to
the voice I might call
on the mental telephone
constructing a story
in some twisted helix way

Trojan Horse

a wooden horse
rolling past stones
the temptation of
arrival was too much
I thought you'd never
haunt me
not even a hint of wind in the trees

your ghost a reduction
thumping in the chest
the painful thrum
reminding me
life isn't an arrow
it doesn't move
in neat progressions
on a Gantt or Pareto
to the waiting executive team
of the soul

it's liquid, eddying
time particles generating a wave
tomorrow as real as yesterday
or as unreal
depending on
how you like your reality

I like mine open
nothing wasted
in the Trojan universe
I'm not afraid
any more
of Greeks bearing gifts

Landscape at Pentecost

after Grace Cossington Smith

Once dreamt
invasion purple
patchwork quilt of scent
tender darkening
as it slopes into evening

what green is this

for exploration
the road leads one way
backwards
behind marbled fingers
hurting springtime
into existence

memento mori

light filters through
horizon coaxes
remember only
this day, this desire.

Irrational Heart

With closed eyes, I watered the weeping
willow you were so proud of
sallow fronds dropping leaves
feather-veined, cultivated
in your final weeks.

Hours wasted
pruning weeds
buffering the shock
those first waves of steely pain
as I watched it wilt.

My hands, covered in dirt
and saw-toothed bracts
hung limply, burning in the sun
waiting to be chastised
by your hovering ghost
as this exquisite tree
which flourished for over a decade
fertilised, nurtured, pruned
to perfection
turned yellow, and slowly died.

A perfect reminder
I didn't need
of failed bargains
and broken promises.

It's a crazy dance
tapping between mask and fist
every muscle twitching
hands in the air
like Ali before he retired
fingers already trembling.

I feint and duck
wondering why you couldn't wait
one year, back then
when time was easier
one more day, now
so I could see you
through your final round.

The buffer of family and friends
fades
moving forward
towards our own inevitable end
as we do.

Only this untempered rawness
when the wash is done, lights off
kids in bed
leather gloves come out
silently punch the wall, which never yields.

How many times
will I pick up the phone
dial the chat we can't have, not even
as we'd joke
on the astral plane.

Instead I walk my dreams alone
hoping to find you there
your body, thin as gossamer
just out of reach.

Perhaps there's time
to pass on dogma
for once
so I can see the angel
sitting beside me while I sort
clothes into three piles
goodwill; keep; give to friends
each piece smelling of
patchouli and nostalgia.

I could wear my own patchouli
stay awake all night, clean the room
bake trays of gritty cookies
anything to negotiate the hurt.

We might pretend in
other parts of space time
that things happen differently
each decision leading to the
moment I lost you
the thin void of energetic space
or patchwork quilt of universes.

If I close one eye, let kaleidoscope
images block the gap
I can picture you, always cold
finally warm beneath
the embrace of that celestial doona.

In the sombre room
we talk for hours
one-sided chatter
that goes nowhere
takes us in tightening circles away
from one another into ourselves
a single point of entry
with no return
the well too deep
too empty of water.

The room itself is unyielding
if I once thought these walls would
expand forever
inflation to the joyful infinity
you spent your life in search of
I was wrong.

It wasn't the open window
you departed by
leaving me here
talking to myself.

It was simple fear
that dark sister you couldn't shake
malignant growth on your shoulder
descending from the amygdala
like a second head
blocking the sunlight
rendering us both mute
me, in all my stubborn life
and you in your
endless death.

An ugly tattoo
written in black and blue
across my skinny arm settles.

Small insects scurry
across the floor
wind moves the blinds
back and forth
as I wait, impatiently.

It's been months now
in this dogged interstice.

Wondering why I still look into the distance
as if there might be a ghost there
smiling and egging me on
you're doing great there girl
just sonorous enough so I'd
know that life isn't
finite as all that
curled like a rabbit
in my pretend womb
but not so loud that anyone else
would know
our little secret
passed across DNA
a mosaic accumulation of scenes, discussions,
layers, skin.

I might share this knowing with my daughter
when she's in need of a god
and no male
armed with a pocket full of tools
will do
tapping our noses against the longing
and feeling just a bit wider
than our thin frames.

If I find enough stillness
I can hear your voice
singing the old lullabies
to get me to sleep
maybe, knowing you
rocking out heaven
or whatever crazy plane
you've gone and inhabited
your songs radiating
through the cosmos
exciting strings we can't see
somewhere in the vicinity
of the irrational heart.

Most of Everything is Nothing

The No Times Times

This is all I know
thrown as confetti
from the birdcage
flying into rusting bars
the inevitable slop of decay.

Oh entropy
here you are, right on cue.

Nothing regains order
without work.

Because of the boundary condition
restraints tighten
as the body crumbles
paradox
driving me to nostalgia
undone in the
expansive past.

Constriction
only happens in the present
which might
from the right stance
be perceived as future
leaving scorch marks with
its invisible arrow
as I try once more
to find time.

Encroachment Spells Erosion

from James Joyce's *Finnegan's Wake*

Annals of themselves
timing the cycles of events
grand and national
makes life work.

The world's a cell
very ordinarily designed
a song of alibi
amid repressed laughter
masculine monosyllables
her enamelled eyes
before she ever dreamt
to spin and grind

That's it.

Laid to rust upon the green
striking the hours
time-killer to his space-maker
in the free of air
when you've bled till you're bone
water on the grave.

I'll bear it on me.

To remind me of
so soft this morning, ours
hides and hints
as if to pass away in a cloud
from ultraviolet to subred tissues
audibly touching
this.

Walking Into Eternity

'Am I walking into eternity along Sandymount strand?' – James Joyce, *Ulysses*

Eyes close into the wind
waves break at your feet
shells crunch to sand
as you observe, soundless
listen, sightless

all things change under pressure
silica and calcium carbonate
call it entropy
that elegant word for chaos
disorder, decay

despite all that
morning brings another sunrise
pink, blue, grey lights reflecting in
winter emptiness

trailing a trawler's net
foetid with memory and superstition
slopping out flotsam
like old fish

a silver gull, kwee-aarr, flies towards the sun
burning the forehead, the retina
your third eye forming ridges
through an awakening mind.

It's enough to walk
full-faced into eternity
gazing from sea to sky to universe.

Life Dreaming

There are days I'd like to live life the other way: a mound of ashes
slowly lifts, impartial, wending around a tissue of molecules
the mental continuum this ceasing, that ceases

taking the span to the end, the dark tunnel sheds no light
green man is just a plant, placed in the corner for extra oxygen
immortality solely divined through the curling deoxyribonucleicacid
in wet eyed children around my bed watching
the clock about to stop, a deep inhale and one final exhale

old age a creeping vine moving slowly through my body
in hot tendrils every stretch aware of itself, the crackle
of bone and joint each day a little less ache, a little more verve
until I'm breathing deeply once more, working my way towards
reversing gravity like time, without panic, knowing
every second where my fingers will land

I pick up pieces of paper, hoping this shuffling
leads to transition as the clock continues to tick
so loudly I'm not sure which way the arrow is flying
or how much time is left before I'm back to parenthood
waves of oxytocin as I put hungry lips to swollen breasts
and lean into the soft density of timelessness where
everything stops in the breaks between contractions

in halcyon thoughtlessness, finding, in the concrete
streets below the double-dutch jump rope a footprint
throwing chin to sky, a secular prayer to calm the pain of change

until the maelstrom begins in desire a primal cry that takes me
back to hyper-conscious singularity every step tentative
each door open any word a state of becoming
a continuity from death to birth, peace to suffering
forever in a state of flux between being and impermanence
finding in this growing emptiness a drop of water spreading
on my, as yet, unformed palm.

Radiology

holding our future in nervous hands
we come with X-rays – icons
in large envelopes with corporate logos

queue for the Delphic Oracle
who divines the auspices
like chook entrails

this arcane analysis
reading the stars within
under cold cathode lights, imaging replacing
ugly imagining
our thoughts digitise into black
and white vaporising to harsh words

I would put those speech
bubbles under their own scan
break down the components
of their dipthongs

meaning as signs
reciprocally determined:
sick/well – a dichotomy sanctioned by the ticking clock
nervous hands melting like a Dali

this arcane analysis
internal astrology.

(collaboration between Magdalena Ball and rob walker)

Maven on Mars

Volatile Evolution
in the tenuous upper atmosphere
Mars' orbit, observed
observing, telemetry
deep space
you are never alone
no matter how dark
or cold.

After that endless journey
orbit insertion
such a clinical
precise entry
to our red neighbour
science-mapping
finding meaning in measurement
composition, structure, escape of gases
life beyond Earth
so strange
but remembering, Maven
we share the same
solar wind
filling our heliosphere.

When your periapsis
deep-dips
almost to the surface
red dust on your pretty spectrometers
won't the selfies flow
like backwards time
your noble attempt to winkle out
where the atmosphere and
water went
just in case something
in those silent, dead strata
might whisper an answer
to our own imminent immolation.

In the Frame

Inside the rectangle
an abandoned swing
cut from a single
piece of wood hangs
off a thick-barked
eucalyptus tree.

It's early spring
just before dusk
light fading to soft green
like the mouldering seat
olive-hued chain, patchy grass
and the forest backdrop
until everything blends
into the dusky teal
of nostalgia.

The woods smell of memory.

Day becomes night
blending into birdsong
bellbird tink, currawong warble
wombat rustling in the undergrowth
natural sounds
outside the frame
without a human referent
over the bench.

The empty swing
remains forgotten
obsolete
in this grown-up world
ageing into nature
alone and persistent
in the frame.

Shallots and Garlic

after *Bawang Merah Bawang Putih*

Every now and then
when the moon is so full it glows green
the wind might howl a lullaby
from another atmosphere.

Then you'll take me by the hand
tell me I'm diligent
show me what to do, and I'll do it
with grace, humility and well.

You'll tell me I'm Garlic, the good girl
heady with the pleasure of service.

But mostly the sky is moonless
no breeze moves the air
you'll know me as Shallots
lazy, sloppy
the ugly sister
I know what I've lost.

Instead of cleaning I'll howl
my dark side out
like a pumpkin full of vipers.

My eyes won't touch the earth
chin too high to kiss.

I'll eat the world and spit it out
licking hungry chops
leaving no bones.

Silence; the coffee cup, the table

'How much better is silence; the coffee cup, the table. How much better to sit by myself like the solitary sea-bird that opens its wings on the stake.' – Virginia Woolf, *The Waves*

The shore the mattress
memory curled in coils
playing as
light on water
air in and out of the room
your eyes in REM
sunk someplace
just out of reach.

Trailing a finger's edge
across purple veins
your breath
incandescent
the warmth of skin
edging consciousness
in kelvin peaks
down my waist
hips, thighs.

Nights seeps
through the cracks
of dreams
into purgatory
this empty room
tastes of illusion
swallowing the sheen of it
the sweet acrid tang
of absence and
wanting more.

Echo Chamber

In the echo chamber
you sat, one leg seductively slung
across today's chair, the other
tapping reverberated Morse code
the song in your head
a doubtful skill
you've never been called to use.

You've got plenty
of those, a database of silent
monkeys, up there, waiting
for their chance.

It wasn't the first time
I found you that way
staring at the phone
lost in the past
your eyes burning my skin.

Your skin shimmered
bioluminescence in the darkness
the warmth of the room
your unwashed beauty
all that talent
wrecking the floorboards
throwing monopoly money
around
inedible confetti.

I almost
wanted to join you
in that fulsome emptiness
lap up the time
weighing heavily
in your open hands.

Most of Everything is Nothing

I wrote a list in blood
taking my time eking out the fantasy

against the full cream of paper edge
colour, sound, light embossing the

surface a recipe that didn't
dull the ache

I watched my tools float
soundlessly down some river

no place you'd have heard of
the empty sky devoid, even of blue

as I knelt one foot in
one foot out of the flow

lifted skin to the sun and prayed
in silent voices

not one, but a multitude taking my
inheritance into a world gone wrong

a thousand years later the river is
clean the paper still white

nothing has changed not even me
a conduit of buzzing atoms

moving by kinetic heat
as I grasp an unwieldy red crayon

with the stubby fingers of a child
and begin to bleed

Six Realms

My death
did the business no good

the mining boom was over
karma was all wrong

extraction and destruction the norm
at the coal face

everywhere the carnage
of bodies

jealousy, the jockeying for power
the air was so grey

I couldn't see the sky
ghosts howled everywhere

I took my things and ran
leaving behind

the hustle and grab
doubt and desire breathing

the harsh smell of fear into my face
rubbery skin against the air

pushing me
away from commerce, security, conformity

the dull smoke-coloured light
from hell still tugged at my groin

even at such a distance
without the anchor of pain

when the wind died
I slowed, eyes rolling back lips soft

all those embers floating, the world
in pale relief and not even surprised

to look behind and find you
licking your lips

chained to your job by that giant hammer
and those endless pockets.

Robin's Eye

Brown Quail (*Coturnix ypsilophora*)

The gentle ker-wee doesn't
break the silence
it blends
a soft grey-brown sound
you might not hear
unless you unplug.

Walk out anywhere
any morning
or that moment dusk becomes night
the best time for walking
close your eyes and
open into the music
vibrating beneath your skin.

From the overgrown grass
at the edge of the forest
behind your house
whistling through your dreams
shuffling in the bush of your
imagination.

I watch for hours
this scrape in the ground lined with grass
small, plump, mottled and plentiful
at the backdrop of my mind.

How is it this bird
has suddenly become visible
for the first time
wearing shades of black
white, chestnut
sharing seed in the covey
moving fast, in stealth
pretending abundance
promising
it is not in decline.

The mournful two-note
tu-wieep
tells another story.

Coral Composition

'It is understood by this time that everything is the same except composition and time, composition and the time of the composition and the time in the composition.' – Gertrude Stein

If I capture
underwater motion
in air
set for decoration
just so

would it push
understanding
through composition
fingers playing
soft-bodied polyps

photosynthesis weary
fish glut
in wild pigment
zooxanthellae
disintegration
into hyperbolic pseudospheres
so striking
they bruise your heart

how could I leave out
crown-of-thorns
bleached
broken reef
swaying
to fractured
music

if I capture just so
if I show you
in the air
if it hurts you
when you touch it
would you still
forget, when it's gone
the meaning of
coral.

Alien World

And what of water?

Simple old H_2O
clear liquid stuff
you drink every day.

Most abundant compound
on the earth's surface
sea water
water vapour, ice
70% of the human body.

You know all that
yet, licking moist lips
you also know
the habitable zone
depends on liquid water
just enough warmth
Goldilocks.

Down here of course
we take it for granted
slurp with abandon
drip down the chin
spray the car
waste without a
second thought.

Drink now
slowly
with knowledge
that throughout the universe
aliens everywhere
your stardust relations
thirst.

Roseanna

for Esther Abrahams

I didn't go looking for infamy
in a handful of black lace.
Embroidered silk thistles and bells
buried in dirt's memory.

You talk of destiny, Roseanna
founder, pilgrim, convict
meaningless names.

The person who was me is gone
my bones reabsorbed
into the air you breathe
the blood that yet pumps through your veins.

Like all women I was many things
mother, thief, lunatic, Jew.

In the end
there's only the helix
generation to generation
the green of your eyes, soft curl of your hair.

I left the rest at Newgate
including my heritage, such as it was
the dust separating me from my people.

My ghost runs lightly over this place
orange light on purple grass
everything angular, constructed
vanities of the living.

Is it vanity to choose such a name?

My mother's, your daughter's daughters
the clock that ticks away from us now
the twisted thread that binds us.

As if the memory of bones
could speak
bringing back a hot, unfertile country.

What I found and what was left

ten thousand miles
from that crowded city
energy, substrates, and
your fat father.

I shed ten skins into the ocean
the sea you never saw
though you were there with me, Roseanna
my girl, you're still there
breathing in and out.

It's only men that lust for power
rum and fiats, laws and empires
hungry always for more
restless with important work.

I survived the journey
laughing down these gilded halls
six squirming babies
under my arms.

By then I was sleeping
on lace, drowning in lace
I wasn't lacking the power women want
the glossy lace of black hair and eyes
suckling my breasts
digging deep into the dirt I now owned.

While you look for my image in faded photos
crackling letters, tarnished silver
here I am.

Deep below the footfall and laughter
children at the gatehouse
a whisper of wind, a sunny Sydney day.

I remain
a voice that can't be silenced.

Can you feel me now
as you swallow
birdsong and willow shift
slipping in and out of oblivion.

Reflecting sphere

Lean in close
fingers hard against lines
mocking tessellations
your skin in honeycomb
decline.

Slather on dioxane, mercury
petroleum, lead
thick as honey.

When you think no one listens
a soft moan escapes
moving slowly
through the atmosphere.

There's no need
to gloss up
airbrushed into oblivion.

All the riches of periodic table hotpot
the scale of atoms and molecules
forged 14 billion years ago
exploded into space
carbon, oxygen, nitrogen
define you.

You are, chemically
already a star.

The Happiness Project

After dark
light slips through
in currents
instead of optics
trailing the length of road
the old school, lost boys
searching for happiness
in rotting nooks
where wood softens
to dust and dirt.

If you're quiet enough
you can taste it
sticky on the lips
like violets or mastic
tears of chios
feel them melting there
distilled essence
like your potions
diluted to x strength
treating like with like.

Nothing of the original remains
just the memory
bittersweet resins
shiver in your mouth
a pain
you can't drink away.

Is it enough?

The sting of life
against absence
layers of longing
slicking the marble
of your headstone.

Ascetic Stitch

There's an ascetic stitch
at the centre of my chest
old, graceless
still throbbing.
It's hard to trace the origin
but I know it has to do with
those flaky croissants
neglected, with the jam
butter, chocolate spread
left for no one
on the kitchen table.

We share our affliction
most keenly
in the kitchen.

All the licking and hoarding
counting the chews
checking for preservatives
and other poisons
feeding and failing
blurring the lines
between parent and child.

I keep pretending I'm different.

Fear fashioned itself into
a well-stocked fridge
a cupboard loaded
with uneaten food
in the event of
the unseen, anticipated
bogyman
finally arriving.

He arrived all right
but by then
you had no appetite.

Cruel Fortune

When was it you handed me that broken cookie with its flapping paper tail?

I held it to my ear, like a conch shell
heard, against the odds, the sea
roaring like a backdrop to our dinner
fortune tickling lobe
hope splashing the shore of my head
like breaking waves.

Mott Street dim sum
the world our fortune cookie
beautiful diners glittering
like immortals
dressing up the room
drinking too much
you on wine at midday
me, always the prude
drowning in jasmine tea
burning cigarettes
like miniature suns
promising so much
leaving so little.

Pursue your dreams
with vigour
you read, again and again
like a shiny phonograph
that pretty mouth
shooting smoke rings
going on and on
in my dreams.

I had no idea how risky
it was
what hubris, taking fortune
into my lips
letting crumbs stain
my best silk
while you slipped
with no warning
out the door.

Robin's Eye

An abruption, against the storm
do you? Quantum tunnelling.

Transported across the barrier of our
cells, the question
I want to ask, stuck.

Meanwhile the car's in
drive, down the empty
freeway, dawn breaking open.

Clouds retracting
night a broken fragment
left behind, in memory.

The car becomes prison
reeking of petrol and want
beetling to nowhere.

Arriving is not the point
you'll never see it, this sweet
vision, honeysuckled.

Clearing at tunnel junction
violating causality
gives way, will you?

Outside the window, the forest thickens
dapples packets of energy
into fruit, leaves, vines: a world.

As if it were your doing
captured light plays likes
protein in a robin's eye.

As you lick the loamy grit
tongue pressed flat against the earth's
angle, magnetic field guiding flight.

Watch the way my mouth moves
borrowing energy
crossing the barrier.

Mirror Neurons

Last night, while everyone slept
I went crawling
with the night creatures

the ground was alive, leaves
shuffling in cinematic motion
thigmonasty on the ground

sentience was a weight
I tried to drop
holding my breath
leaning into the thistles

I slid off my skin and sank
lips stretching open
tree frog croak
joining the chorus

a tiger quoll
stalked its prey
white spots flashed against

darkening cold, ants and crickets
raising an alarm
nocturnal solitude halted

I gave into eucalyptus crunch
choir of bats, owls, wuk-wuk
licked my lips and tasted black soil

loamy grit in the teeth
vegetation below my body's heft
I was the earth, the sky

meanwhile, in the silent
sleeping house
the pale flickering screen tried
and failed
to mirror these neurons.

Old Wounds

It was the day after the day
you nearly strangled
the dog pushing her
into the dirt my eyes bulged
lips glued tight while
you shouted
keep up.

I don't think it's possible for skin
to get any whiter than mine was
kabuki white, though strictly
speaking shades of white are
actually neutral greys: death grey
the absence of colour.

Colour is a private sensation
anyway, like fear.

In the now of what some might call
aftermath a pattern of broken molecules
appears in the gravel below
yesterday's feet while I fall further
behind atoms vibrating harder in the
centre while the edges of my life spread

into this new space, charged by
discomfort
every day, it's like a new start
into an old wound.

Circus Factory

under the bridge
that day
urine and loneliness
perfumed the air
after the show
that weird twist in the gut
when the music stopped
graffiti and rust

walls melted against
the forward shuffle
feet through time
decomposing branches linking
lives layered
against our chests

beating a hungry rhythm
walkers, jugglers, broken tent pegs
into the past
an exhibition of pain

a carousel
you'll never ride
forever reaching for
that ring thing
the pink squeak
of cotton candy
achingly sweet
in its absence
at the back of your jaw

Mobius Strip

Every day I get closer to the gap.

Each moment my goodbye repeats in Möbius strip zero
twisting around itself and back to the start

I am told there are an infinite number of topological
embeddings haven't we been here

before, the absent warmth of your presence
three dimensional memory charging space

alone against the silence of your voice
pressing me on

in that loop against disorientation, my boundaries
scaffolding the helix wrapped phantom cry

the house shakes with your mass
though you weighed so little in the end

it was almost an impossibility, all those dualities
especially love, that bastard son of collapse

I didn't know the other side was mere simulation
simulacra generate more simulacra: the model I keep building

a sweater I keep knitting, and unknitting
the same coat you made to keep me warm

chills me as I crawl, an unborn child, blind and hungry
back around the fold towards this place of darkness
this gap.

Television, the sea, the window

It's like real sand, shell grit grains between the toes
real seahorses and crabs, virtually real
who knows what's real anyway
in this augmented life dreamt in flashes through the window.

All you ever wanted was an authentic taste
salty sea tang against your tongue
biting back blood from waterlogged lips.

If I told you this was truth would you swim for me
long hair flowing against the current, feet paddling hard
with no fear of drowning, no fear of anything.

In sine wave immersion the birth of a beach
signals take shape in teal blues moody grey
paint cracking on glass for breadth and depth.

These hands stretch pushing against the tide
paddling towards your lonely new world
television and dysphoria, a flickering light like dawn.

You've always been the video star, no matter where
you find your body: behind or in front of the camera
the painted box complete, in this space of
morning and broken solitude.

Cold Mirror

I wasn't sure how to approach this thing
finding it there in the middle of all my sorrow
suspended in the cooling light of dusk

it wasn't so much familiar as intimate
dangling tentacles in hot orange
boldface against the dusky ocean
falling upward into my daydream

you might have been there
as you're everywhere
a peek-a-boo phantom dropping by
to check my progress, or otherwise

in non-binary bloom against a fizzing heart
harpoon sting of loss
lingering as phenomenon
I tried to touch its bell-pulsing beauty

fingers slipped through to paper
streamers of optic illusion, a cold mirror
reflecting the spectrum
cold comfort for an embrace

not so much alien
disappearing just when I'd begun to soften
as fragile whispers and pulsation
memory's filter breaking perception

transmitting a message
in transient heat
just beyond infrared.

Harnessing Wind

I'm done with cast iron alibis, wind turbines
moving anticlockwise against half-articulated desires

no matter how many promises are thrown around
it's always the same, pinwheels hang like paper cuts
when we knew how to generate energy
taking warmth from the summer sun

I don't know the reason
for the energy
or where it gets used
look closer and you'll see
your own face there, spinning

I could dry these water drops in a towel, breathe in
the sea salt while you move in tighter circles
harnessing wind, a seagull flying backwards
into time's breeze to find what we lost
that sharp, familiar song cutting through static
a wash of water over black rocks
Neptune's Necklace

intertidal motions push against
barriers of skin
the sand beneath sky
so many spaces between clouds
we might fly upward
forever, buoyed aloft by hundreds
of plastic whirligigs
a forest of peppermint toys
in which
I'm ready now to believe.

Migration

As the tundra melts
assumed history reveals itself
methane bloomed
carbon mounted
intersteller dust
like woodchip traces
of a family tree
left behind, returning.

All those years of staring
into the grey-mottled sky to read
the signs, another world
driving me forward
to human space
a secret past curled like an ovum
in the womb.

Buildings rise higher in dreamscape
zodiac cloud seed comets
charge the night air in longing
and terror. It could be the source
reaching for a voice
egg spawn arrow bane
to finally take this pilgrim
home.

Decoherence Through the Window

Sometimes it's all about the window.

You do everything right, playing
a finger along the dusty ledge
follow the manual without fail
colour in the lines just so
still the window remains closed
all the good stuff
happening outside the pane
life suffers
in the spaces between a blue wall
a pink floor.

The orange recess stays shut
two dimensions.

Destination looks like an opening.
Thick crosses of certainty
hint at the full Mardi Gras, what
feathers and flowers you might be
missing on this side as you edge
forward in time
listening for music
beyond the frame.

Until the moment you open it
probability waves
a fluttering hand
the tightly packed microscopic
pixels remain unlimited
possibilities surrounding you
multifoliate, like energy.

Inanimate

I had a meeting with the rocks
in the frail hour of dusk
prone
my body
given up to mineral.

Bony fingers traced mottled
green moss, pits and crevice
like braille, speaking through
intent and sign, like old friends
this igneous communion
bringing me back to elemental.

My whiteness was ghostly shame
a badge I wore as skin
weathering into the earth
merging into darkness
forming and reforming.

They told me
not in so many words
that I was older than I looked
that all things
even the inanimate
responded to compassion.

Dark Matter Wants to be Alone

How far would you go
in the darkness
slowly towards the end of the road
where the path splits
to parallel lines
one leading away
somewhere icy and free
the other crunching leaves
beneath bare feet
bird songs you recognise
smells to say
you're heading home.

Is it wrong to want warmth
to choose the safer route
a quiet so deep it cancels thought?

Reaching for stolen protection
butter knife and china plate
the mother-urge; motherlode
and everything that pulls
like gravity, against
your resisting body.

Relief comes in bursts of sunlight
short-lived, curated, absorbed
and lost, returning to
this fork in the road.

The solemn unknown
inferred rather than observed
sliding invisibly, exerting
the slightest of pressures
molecules interact with air
night breeze sinks against rising heat
reaching into the silence
to touch those spaces
that remain open
visible only
through a missing electrical charge.

As dark matter's mysterious ghost
I inhabit two worlds
feed two hearts, hedging bets
just in case one proves to be real
the beater; the keeper.

Angel

'In the moonlight, who are they, cross-legged,
telling their stories over and over?' – Carl Sandburg, 'Dogheads'

This all-too-human brain, weighed down neural structures and metacognition
always chugging and puffing, a locomotive moving too fast towards no
destination, as if elsewhere were evolution, future trumping present, each
moment instantly demoted to memory, adding noise.

For you no grudge can take hold, the past might never have
existed, distracted into joy by a soft hand against your heaving
stomach, three hundred million olfactory receptors ready for action
and a belly full of devotion.

I could meet you there, throw all this chaos out
with the dirty bathwater, do nothing that doesn't count
as play, work being a construct made by people
meaningless dogma in the dull thud of sunshine
a ball pushed against the leg, an itch.

Is it enough to just be, where stories are always present tense
food a silver bowl endlessly filled
where no responsibility takes precedent
over a diggable patch,
a bone, and attention.

A Cloud Withdrew

Mapping Pluto

In the corner of my eye
crude patterns of dark and light winked behind
averted vision, engaged the cones and rods
of my retina as a shadowy silhouette
then gone.

Not for the first time.

When I was no older than four or five you were
there, question mark on your chest
like a slogan T-shirt, appearing from the dreamworld
whispering my name when no one
else was answering the phone.

In the lean years
your celebrity reduced to dark glasses and exo-status
I tried to keep you close through long nights
thrashing in my hallucinations
the nightmare of your voice, muted music
Holst's Renewer, unwritten, unknown
like a true god of the underworld.

Let's not pretend you're nameless
hovering just there, in the ICU
lurking like an unwanted friend
against the metal tang of machinery
monitors, ventilators, keeping life going
while you wait, wait, always waiting
for the soft touch of flesh.

When I finally find you, looking
directly into your dark face
tenderly tracing bony cheekbones with my fingers
alien scent against my skin
will I feel this same hot longing
hollow pain driving my hands to knit and unknit
or will I know you implicitly
all the geysers, craters, moons and rings mapped
familiar as a welcome home.

Absences

I'm in your house again
all windows open
the kettle on
tea for one
my company not augmented
by your ghost
courted, coaxed and
called
while silence echoes
off the walls.

I'm not really there
but your ghost bleeds
through the rooms
trailing my lacuna with milky
vapour, like ghosts do
all ectoplasm and wind
your body given up to longing
ten thousand miles
away and across time
the pull
distorts my skin
spots and lines
appear like surface features
rising against gravity
while you howl
from nowhere.

In the midway point
where I always hoped
we'd meet
fingers clasping, eyes linked
I know that face like my own
every haggard edge
each whispering touch
a deeper absence.

Stargazy

Oh luminous sphere of plasma
tell me now
let's not mess about
I could get a crick
craning towards the sky
while I wait for an answer.

In the end, we're all like you
burning up our fuel
collapsing after what feels like
ten thousand years
give or take
in the relative forever.

Flawed and yelling
I stand on heavy legs
star bound
Just an ordinary
hydrogen-burning fool
scratching out my final
glowing moments
beneath an atmosphere of dust
and a canopy of eucalyptus
poor shade
while I look to
the Milky Way
with love and
envy.

Mourner's Kaddish

for Eve

I woke this morning with you in my eyes, expansive as
always, with that frilly floral apron, carrying a
tray of something nourishing while I held myself back like
a hungry dog knowing this gift was illusion, your door
no longer open to me, even though my need was great.

You appeared so welcoming, 1940s hair black and
curly, lips painted Ava Gardner red, waist cinched below
the smock, sexy at sixty-five, cheeks glowing, laughing that
raucous laugh up and down the music scale, and I could swear
you were here, your breath filling the room moving over the
old pine table and chipped cups with that irreverent (a
word, for some reason, you could never pronounce), impatient
cackle that convinced me you'd save my ass once again; that
you were (of course) immortal and that I had no business
crying like this.

The smell of coffee hits me with the impact of my Kaddish.
I wanted to put flowers on your grave but I didn't
know where you were buried; you never liked cut flowers
anyway: the mess, your hay fever, the waste of money.
Though you've been gone over two years I feel the darkness you
conceal beneath your perfectly made up eyes, emotion
tamped into song: cry me a river, baby.

I try to conjure your face during those last weeks when I sat by your bedside, apologising, holding your cold smooth hand, fingers misshapen by arthritis; try to find your bare face, eyes closed in dreamless sleep, but I can't.

For me you'll always be in motion, standing in the bright light of your kitchen, the percolated aroma, cut cake, a ready joke. If I close my eyes and whisper this prayer of thanks for your abundance, for teaching me the meaning of home; as day dulls into evening, I might find you here once more, filling the corners of my kitchen, laughing the music scale, irreverent, immortal (of course), and singing me home.

Unmaking Atoms

Yesterday you said goodbye
for the third time
your breath lifting
the hair on my neck as you
whispered another vow.

I watched you leave
your lips barred, arms bridged
against an unyielding chest.

I've kept track of these
farewells
a book by the bedside
scribbling invisible letters
while I blank my face.

When you return
your breath is shallow
the bed colder than wind
but we pretend it's warm
wake in silence
words hidden in the ledger of loss.

Because I'm a woman
I know you're right
it's my habit of hiding
meaning in parcels
beneath my skin.
If you reached out a finger
you'd find them
swollen against the veins
releasing a strange scent:
musk and sadness.

You said goodbye again
maybe it was just an ordinary wave
a little post-coffee blood
pieces of flesh
I might pick up while I wash
dirty dishes, tidy the counter.

I don't know how to share
other than secretly
in lemon juice ink
knowing every word unspoken
is one step closer to the one
that sticks
the one that will unmake these atoms.

A Cloud Withdrew

Emily Dickinson redaction

A cloud withdrew
from the sky
forever lost
secured in the glow
of hermetic memory.

It's the nature of clouds
slippery like liquid
to disappear after seduction
leaving no trace
Ars Memorativa
though I know it was I
who let you go
feeling so strong
while you found
your elemental self
water vapour
my face wet
the sky empty.

To never
pass the angel with a glance
and a bow
firm in my intention
finding you only through
redaction
the spaces between my fingers
association
the phantasm that evokes
emotion.

Venus in the East Before Sunrise

The light this hour is shrill
leaves underfoot
shades of ochre
browns and pinks
the memory of night
warm beneath their spines.

Usually morning comes
with its promise
anything might happen
mostly, but not today
where the sun wanes
before it begins
dawn is oily and slow
every step hurts the breath

I move with purpose
as if nowhere were
a spot in the distance
at the end of the road

wondering if that silvery disk
just beyond the tree
is Venus
and why and in what way
it matters

that bright spot
almost within reach

no shell-covered Roman goddess
rising wet and ready
as if you could ascribe gender
to such a world
volcanic, angry
heady with atmosphere
ashen lit
a wild greenhouse below thick
stable clouds of microbes
uninviting
still beautiful.

Portfolio

The market's down, boys
better wind in your portfolio.

The rest of us can
hide in the kitchen
steaming in our coffee mugs
listing our assets, just in case.

For spare change
you can count
blessings
written in black texta
over peeling paint.

You could get high
on that cresol
making decisions
on the whiteboard
then rubbing them out
ink all over your shaking hands.

Don't forget to
lick up the biscuit crumbs
before you leave
so no one
knows you were here.

Weather Situations

Last month, it was all drought.

We'd gotten used to restrictions
unending heat, throat-constricting dryness
leaves crunching
in husked shades
beneath desiccated spines.

We rationed our drinks
tended a wilting garden
watching for embers in
the crackling sky.

In the morning
light-headed with thirst
we danced for rain
in dust, hoping
our inartistic thumpings
might influence
the atmosphere.

The weather responded
with a palinode
a developing low
gale-force southeasterly
bringing more rain
than anyone bargained for
flooding the road
bloating the creek beds
the sky ugly and bruised.

In the silence of our blackout
mocked by howling wind
and trees swaying
too much for comfort
you gurgled, saturated in the
living room,
extreme is
the new normal.

Pranayama

Through this morning's breath practice,
I would recreate you, like a homunculus
one inhalation at a time
in desperate constriction
gasping as you would have done
near the end, holding on
until there was
only
one
more
wheeze.

All
paths
lead
to home
even the most twisting
in ragged *pranayama*
holding your awakening tongue
between the teeth slowing down the
fire that took you
finding expansion the ocean of your re-arrival
animated by memory and movement
forgiving, with each transition
the breath that failed you
the heart that hurt you
into stillness.

Inside Your Darkest Everything

'A harp and a Jacaranda were the music' – Frida Kahlo, 'Memory'

i

When I came to
I was alone
under the jacaranda
the sky an evil purple
threatening to break

I held tight to the scaly trunk
for stability
and wondered

the world had shifted during the long night
your pain settling into my organs
inside the darkness spread
black ink flowed through my veins
pumping blood into the lungs

in three dimensions
there was muted colour
fractured through a prism
everything broken up
dispersed into elements.

ii

Your eyes were bigger
than I remembered
heavy lidded without glasses
long plaits wrapped on your head
in flowers
emulating Frida again
your mirror twin
be-costumed and sharp
incorporeality no impediment
to the rousting march of your
big red boots.

As for me, I sat in the shadows
neither one thing nor another
trying desperately to make you
live again
a woebegone Doctor Frankenstein
pale with longing.

iii

In wavering tones of ombre
you beckoned
strumming a harp
the blue house, the yellow chair
your hair suddenly alight
a halo of orange flames
crackled and burned.

Your laugh shook the floor
Día de los Muertos
as you dragged my arm
skin electric against
the shock of touch
heart exposed
like a vivisection
beating time.

Somehow, together
we drove your
beat-up car
on the wrong side
of consciousness
moving too fast down Market Street
the wood facade
of Woollen Mills Chapel
peeled open its doors
offering a peace we might
take up like pilgrims
if we weren't so damned
secular, though I
wanted to believe
in something, anything
I was ready to
chant, *sit shiva*
do whatever it might take
to make this wild
goose chase
down cobblestones
real.

iv

I know this place, its corners
the dull scent of memory
that lingers on the drapes
the cheery sofas and pillows
the flameless candles that
outlived you.

On the rack by the front door
a neat row of shoes
that won't be worn again
waiting, forever
for a foot
to animate them.

On the wall, a framed print
magnolias surrounding
a prickly pear cactus flower
the lurid buds
stare me down
proud, in spite of their
ridiculous ephemerality
another layer that takes me
through the canvas
into all that was concealed
corseted, controlled
inside the lines
the perfect silence
those places a child
never sees.

Hieroglyphics

Autotopography

This is the space I find
shaping my body
around corners
smoothing fingers into plaster
pushing flesh against walls
a cosy place for telling.

I couldn't go there now
with so many barriers
to travelling, the city too far
the cost, astronomical.

So when you said, come
I tried but I
I stuttered against
your call I
didn't have the address
of course I should have known
the white box of clay soil
was mine, the landscape
rich with microorganisms
my own flora
making up the three dimensions
you inhabit
with the grace of dreams.

The room before me
forever locked
made too long ago
in breathless puffs of polluted city air
the walls licked
smooth as adobe
crab-walking back and forth
in designer shades
the curtains just so
vivid Marimekko, let's say
above a grey day
full of so much noise
it's almost silence.

I could go there maybe
see you again
in the orange and green floral
flap of cotton against a warm
night breeze
if it weren't for the outrageous cost.

Dhurbar Square

When the rain finally came
clouds breaking into tears
above cracked walls
soil softened into rivers

I saw you, in Kathmandu
as I see you everywhere
hands trailing, fingers spread
starfish through the rubble

without you here
nothing is the same
the keyhole lock swings outward with
no key no door no wall no floor

we buy time in imaginary spaces
the gaps between breath
the sand shift of concrete
your eyes, those endless wet windows
open to silent rumble
where there's no time

this is your secret journey
a landscape of emptiness
of fullness, transformation
the left-handed path

your feathers rise
poison in your beak
brightens the plumage
rainbow body, earth to water
water to wind

all I know: the taste in
my mouth says find you
find you find you

and I find you
waking again
incomprehensible
in boundless light.

Energy Conservation

What is it about morning
breaking the membrane
of dreams, a pile of splinters
flood of light thrusting me outside
away from woodsmoke and sleep.

When you came to, I was already gone.

My body lost its dark solidity
the tender heat
you sought
foot shuffling beneath the doona
was a blank space interstice.

In the wild opening
water flowed through
fissures, moss-flocked
a particle zoo
breaking symmetries
horizon-stretched
testing the boundaries
of skin, the flexibility of bone
molecules in
motion dissolving into earth
reaching towards sky.

What was soft, yielding, lost in sorrow
emerged as stone, marble, wood
a Bangalow palm, fronds open to the sun.

You'll never find me
though I'm everywhere
you are.

Hieroglyphics

After the Online at MoMA exhibition http://www.moma.org/
interactives/exhibitions/2010/online/#works

i Surface Tension

Don't ask why the surface tension
broke, a whirlwind of charcoal whipping
us towards something we couldn't control

in serpentine motion, blossomed outwards
floral blooms tricking the light
the warm wind opening

this wasn't what you asked for; not what you ordered
your eyes closed against my fingers
while we prayed together soundless Kaddish

our whispers dissolved to blueshift
decreasing in wavelength sliding to redshift
a twist like longing, vibrating voice of light

once I separated the object from its referent, laid
out in careful mosaic, the place, the plane flattened
stopped, like the clock, the point of measuring, not the point

it wasn't quite your instrument, but something like
string twisted, wood distorted, cardboard, wire
a toy really, but the sound was pure and clear, no faking

that's where I lost you, your hand slipped, breath exhaled
to void, the word I won't say not even as euphemism
at the border, bypassing past, rewriting in tattered news

the hieroglyphics undid me, body unhinged in a
nightclub, the white of my dress becoming the room
disengaged from the flesh beneath transforming space.

ii   Line Extension

Moving beyond the flatline, a dialogue between
dimensions rises, falls in intonation, one step removed
your third eye follows me, surprise lurking in every corner

air currents flow against the ghost of your spine
reaching for a line of energy, a memory you can't quite
shake, even after all this time

colour mapped on colour, layered in lines of trust
deep into your surfaces, umber on red it could be one shade
or many, motion against stasis

a tightrope high-wire balancing this moment with that
straining towards the prize, the fish at hook end
though there's no fish here, no hook, nothing but the line

your damaged collage, flocked, removed, x'd out
scraps, cobbled in haste before you before
age drove us apart, before you fell into this no space

a slow flash of copper, lightning sundial
opens an abrasion, broken layers of skin peel back
the story becomes hybrid

entangled, unfolding in extended bridge
the string stretching its dimension
line to line, finger to finger emerging

absent body dancing along the nervous
system, spinal chord vibrating, neural cross-connections
sliding down the triangular, gone but somehow still here.

iii   Confluence of line and plane

I want to understand these cloudy signs
walking the line of resistance
travelling the length of my body, feeling forward

when I reached the scaffold of cubic repetition
I started to run, it was too open, devoid of logic
a tangle of pumping circles against angles

all possibilities had been exhausted once I reached orange
there was nowhere else to go, except through
to unknown planes, gasping, arrested by your scent

at that confluence, things were changing
the shift tectonic, loss dispersing
breaking down to pattern, texture, shadow

the rings of a tree trunk
overflowing out of the tree
ridges of skin, segments of life

the story you've left in me
a ridge against the inside
scar tissue

like art, I could make myself in positive integers
on carbon, memory cutting figures across a black expanse
as I move through these places, at grand scale

finding a tincture of who you were
each detail of your absence, bringing back
the line and curve that makes us whole.

Unchanging unceasing murmur

It always begins with this
withal, the missing parts,
and the cold wind that bit

in no part did I stop to
complain, warm, rewind
this path of no where

underneath a verandah
of possibilities
inked, unforgiving
like the migrant that I am
always on the run
always remaining
in place

neither this nor

in the morning you
tried to warn me
the stars were still out
not counting sol
the day held some kind of promise
as most days do
your heathen heat
like so many practices
offered temporary comfort
the solace of stretching
a wood fire
deep breath in
and exhale

then on the run again
tracked between
the pots and pans
clashing like wild dogs
in the kitchen
the bucketing rain
that never stopped, even
when the sun shone

the fire had gone out
the door was still open
my unmarked flesh
discarded
on the new sofa.

Nature's Observatory

In the season of hot wind
the air took your breath
a reverse offering
under the verandah
at night
when busy diurnals
gave way to a slow silver-grey
ooh ooh ooh of
tawny frogmouth

plain time comes flooding
with the water
in intervals
there's at least one
each year that binds us here
a reminder
that hurrying is futile
we all end up the same
loam, soil, earth
the itch that can't be scratched
solitude
those flowery slopes
smiling in dark light
candle drawn and unwashed
as we roll the dice
again

the morning
comes early this time
I find myself alone
my back against the mountain
looking at my hand so hard
it hurts, just a little
all these lines
against the light
your unread books
in situ on the bedside
next to the clock
the swell of your missing
chest
the beating
heart, the heat

I haven't heard that sound
for a while
crackle of sun on the roof
an unassuming whoop-a-whoop
green and brown canopy
the present constantly updating itself

back door open
to the wild
unknown

and now, in the space of your
absence, my breath tastes
the brush of that scent
woody-sweet camphor
eucalyptus
the ground thick with bark
leaves, remnants of
last season's storm
cleans my sinuses
clears illusion, your softness
congealing in the oils
against a pressed palm
lingering
long past the touch of your skin
on my skin.

Woman with her hair loose

There's a slip down the centre line
where water becomes ice becomes water
when it's melting

I'm the woman with her hair loose
looking at you
in the foreground
a green backdrop
superimposed over pastoral
rising in wave motion
from Antwerp oil

nothing but this space
could touch you
the rest driven back in time
heartstop point on the canvas
that lies, and tells
and lies again

look at the way the world
disappears, down by the creek
mapping the angles of memory
a shade through the undergrowth
your mouth
saturated in colour
working in rhythmic lines
recreating
the traces in your brain
just another construct
dimming in the evening light

when you find me
my eyes are implacable
though the rest is all softness.

Entopic Imagery

Man those colours
are arresting
at the periphery

corner of the eye
phenomena
shadow ghosts
a turquoise ocean
back then
sea bubbling into memory
sky finding sun
scattering wavelengths of blue
leaving only the red

that time and this time
the drop of water hits the sea
pulls up in ribbons of moon
shock of recognition
too much like longing

it isn't what we see
when we look out
the window
organic forms
the whip of wind
night moving in
as if the moon were really white
clouds curling into sheep
salt on the lips

it's night
somewhere now

this striking light
might heal us
if only we can perceive it
like this
red on blue
softer than the cut of love.

Probability Waves

the end is so close
I can smell it
red candles
glowing in the distance

here's what I won't do

you're watching
in your singularity chair
thin body
cushioned
against the blows
a stupidly short life
there's nothing pretty
in that
move along boys

there are some places
even a poet can't go

here's what I don't want
to hear: love, laughter, hope
it's too close
a lazy threat
hovering near the
border
no-man's-land versus
the shock of morning

don't open the door

if I never know
then all things are possible.

Essential Whites

Writing this way, while waiting for transition is like the swipe of a hand against my face: that blessed sting. When you finally wake I can't find the threshold. My eyes had grown into marbles, legs stiff from pacing the room. The windows open and shut, two more hungry mouths. Little by little it becomes a game: I pick you pick, leaving tiny scars that are somehow soothing later in the closet with the door shut. Because the light is off, it's too dark to see the marks though I know them to be red half moons against the white of my wrist: Savage Silk, Bianca, Bombe Alaska. I think of the 'essential whites' paint pots we tested, lined in a neat row, like children waiting to be stroked. I feel the inverted bumps beneath my fingers as I touch them tenderly. There's something almost warm about this place of ice which is no place, where I wait for the knock, wait for change, now, when everything has inexplicably failed. It's a cocoon in here, halted at the point of inhalation, with you out there, not knocking. But I know, I can taste, that you're coming this way.

In Situ

When I arrived she had already begun the process
it was sometime later, but nothing had changed
there was much to do, but nothing more to be done
the air smelled strongly of incense, now forever connected
my brother chanted, penance for a petulant youth
there was no progression; there could be no progression
after all the effort, we could do nothing
the air was thick with silence, hunger, and too much food
it was cold, but the windows stayed open
the windows were open, but no air came in
we were stifling with cold
she didn't look peaceful but everyone said so
a grimace is not a smile
the house was full of people, but it was silent
comfort was everywhere, but barren
there was nothing to do; we were very busy
cleaning, packing, putting away: winter approached
after that, no one spoke
nothing was resolved
it was not a neat ending
it was not a beginning
it felt unnatural, as if it hadn't happened
it was the natural order of things
everyone said so
and left, smiling, empty containers in hand.

Gargantua redacted

I must refer you
do not take it ill
remembered
more delectable

lick his slipper
a crafty chuff
from the depth
where they fish for roaches
in the bottom of his fur

rags of parchment
under the rainbow
a-bird-catching
her duck below

Cheer up your hearts
on the dagger

farewell muses

taking and receiving
in this ritual

that intellectual sphere
whose centre is everywhere
circumference nowhere

hidden underground
not without reason

forcing thunder
on your hemisphere
good illustrious lantern.

Velocity or Pause

RNA World

I watched the house martin
lift its wings and fly
for the first time
blue head and sharp tail
fluttering off the freshly
painted fence: the thing it
was born for.

In this transition, young
became old
a one-way
direction from helpless
to independence to helpless again.

The mud pellet nest under the
eaves fell into disuse.

My ageing body pushed
onward in the same ordering
principle that Eddington said
was a property of entropy
alone.

The bird came back
again that day
or maybe another year
an accidental coincidence
or not, it's eye calmly
refracting my bulk into
sound, shock waves
and heat,
recognising
the RNA world
that preceded this one:
our common ancestry.

I pulled
against the flow
in hopeless gesture
shifted, transformed,
lifted aching wings and flew
towards dissolution
until I no longer felt
heartbeats below my chest
the tick-tock motion of
hammock and sunrise.
The curtains blew inward
sunlight reshaped the roof.

The bird's motion was illusory
a continuous flow from known
to unknown.

The tears that fell
on my paperbark skin
dried before they reached
their destination.

Velocity or Pause

'Eternity will be
Velocity or Pause'
– Emily Dickinson, 'Two Lengths has every Day'

By the waterside
below the rocks
of another midnight moon
she waits.

That breathing is
no breathing
in and out
like every memory
tightened into one
the velocity of her scorn
moves me forward.

I want to find her
the siren lute
promising peace
once fear is done
but I won't go there.

Instead, I stay warm
legs curled beneath me
the sofa must be safe
yellow chintz
with floral relief
too many pillows
and herbal tea.

The clock looks domestic
enough, slicing through
each hour of this damp
evening, frogs creating
a symphony outside
some group scene
of mayhem
only existing
in the fragile hold
of night.

It doesn't matter what comforts
the house holds.

Time will take me to her
inevitable, she sings
a voice of dirt and silence.

Misinformation Effect

Here's one more wish
planted into solid ground
earth, water, fertiliser
my thumbs remain black

another piss in the
river, fish swim in
these glowing shadows
100 trillion synapses
can't find the
connection

a story of neuroscience
waxy warmth
the scent of cut roses
in a vase on
the table
in your kitchen
flowers gone, the room
non-existent
this cortex on fire

a complex web
encoding/decoding
indelible traces
eye shift, jawline in profile
tilt of the head
a voice like dark milk
drifting in and out

with so much space
between us
would I know you
face to face
in some other form?

Redhead Beach

Arriving, never fully
at this beach
closed due to rough surf
snuck in, an interloper
sand from another time
between these toes

not one molecule
other than the enamel
on my teeth
the cartilage in my bones
remains
from that person
on that beach
but here again
memory finding itself
the water hitting the shore
in patterns fully familiar
the rocky outcrops
shark tower

blue on blue
like heartbreak
your eyes against the ocean
the ocean against the sky

a seagull nods
as if to say
yes, me too
refreshed but not renewed

a network of cellular
connections between neurons
a conduit that survives
even the startling indigo
of that light

alone, always
but never quite
without you.

Winter Apples

let me go there
in the final days
of your fruit
underscored
by late night frost
an empty tree
the season
of my youth

one thousand
years ago
give or take
in the frozen present
like two apples
stubbornly
holding on
while everyone
else has
given in

I feel your breath
cold against
my cheek
taste the sweetness
of that flesh
in its imaginary
freshness
unyielding

Watagan Walk

There was a moment
Mount Warrawolong in view
throat constricted with the effort of climbing
where I stopped thinking about you.

Only fools would work this hard
I heard you say
but it was just wind in my ears
clouds parting briefly for a shot of blue.

Past boulders covered in moss
Illawarra flames, red cedar branches
walking barefoot, my feet treading
lightly on broken promises
like the memory of kinship
a wedge-tailed eagle overhead
eyes squinting against summer sun.

How easy it would be
to reject this gift
that was never mine
an exception to the rule
city girl on the hill
in plastic sunnies and khakis
lips whiter than the
ice cream mountain top.

Yet I call this forest home
find my own handprint
in abandoned caves
recognise goannas blending to bark
the screech of lorikeet and cockatoo
more familiar than a honking horn.

Eucalyptus breath
draws me back
as if it were a return
c'mon it says
your body is earth bound
this soil, this smell.

Free Radicals

I woke into a dream
aged like an old book
my pages yellowed
the narrative unreadable
print faded into patterns
raised veins on the hand
hieroglyphics

the bed shook with fear
but I remained calm
slipping deeper into REM
your breath a wind
against my face
micro-awakening
desire, a small voice
a tear, though nothing
moved in the house
in the room

the dog was barking
a shadow on her brightness
I heard it from paralysis
alarm from the outer world
just enough to
break the windows

in the morning light
I rubbed my arms
skin falling into folds
like fabric drapes

my heartbeat
recounted each break
lip stain on my face
caught between cracks
and knew
it was no dream.

Dogstar

Don't bite there
that's the dogstar
a scar you won't see
because you don't look

smoothing down the edges
sweet talking Jane
in her smithy suit

pour the drink in the
ice bucket
no one will notice
they generally don't

it isn't easy
this smile
it takes work to
arrange it
such blinding whiteness

you don't know
because you aren't here
scrolling till the end
your fingers on autopilot
tapping into some
subconscious
desire
for oblivion.

Lacuna

This time, unlike the
time before, wasn't
especially unique

it was that kind of week
everyone seemed to be going
it was hard not to
take it personally

the air was soupy
all the trees were lying low
no solace in the great
outdoors, just accumulated
beads of sweat

my car wouldn't start
it stuttered along the gravel road
then stopped
like you, mid-sentence

there were no words

just rain
which began suddenly
as if in answer to the
stalled vehicle
the water kept coming
washing my face
mascara memories
black streaks on white skin
the shiver of a cold change
lacuna of your departure

and no sound.

Image of the day

Already it has been one of
those years
people crying in the street
a wailing wall on my way to work
though life continues
we prepare meals, get up, get on
go to bed
repeat

it's easy pain
not like the loss
of someone real

that happens
just once and then
like vaccination
you become immune
no exploding supernova
can unhinge
the solidity of that hole

so why all this moon dust

clinging to images
an ageing child
counting losses
with dry eyes
staring into the night sky

as if somewhere up there
let's just call it up
is an answer
to your departure.

Planet Nine

What would you say
if I were to slip
past the filter, tonight?

I could put something
in place to serve

a replica
doing the dishes
with the same earnest
lack of care, cutting cheese
feeding the dog.

Meanwhile, deflection out of
the ecliptic plane
just past the Kuiper Belt
a long way from my parent star
a long way from anywhere

pad in hand
I could be shortlisting names
Tycho, Sedna, Planet Nine
or something more
evocative to conjure
the particular loneliness
this evening
in the far reaches
of the outer solar system.

I could draw pictures
for no one
in thick lines
pale shades
flatlined through
the frame
pulling other objects
into its orbit

in purple crayon
a real life Harold
drawing the past
holding my chubby
scientific instruments
tightly in the fist
all wrong
the scribble a portal
dominating the night sky.

Fractals of Fractals

There's no escape from math

the same self-similar sound
scaffolded in quasi-continuous
hierarchy

don't say
slow drawl into my ear
that you don't understand

I know you do

your eye twitches
uncontrollably
blinking with the
shock of
knowledge

I wrote this book
myself
at the atomic scale
of pain
the soft splash of blood
offered in repeating
platelets
plasma iterations
into the bag
a long distance gift
that looks just like
itself

all those pieces
of missing time.

Qualia

There's no way
I'm going back there

years haven't covered
everything in rosy patina
a cracked Vermeer of nostalgia
working overtime

it's still ugly
fresh enough to be raw
nets of proteins and
carbohydrates stretch across
every nerve cell
a pattern of lacy holes

held to the past
like a warning
chiming through dark silence

molecules storing those memories
have been destroyed and
recreated thousands of times

I'm not that person
that pain wasn't mine

this I know
like I know that
time and space
are illusions

the sensation of colour
the strength of your hand
against my skinny back
everything in this moment
that's already gone.

Solar Collections

I very nearly missed it

the uneven sky at five a.m.
water rising currents
on morning blasted skin

we were the solar collectors
breaking our vows
in the light
pretending we had
empty hearts

having come so far
it would have been foolish
to leave at such an early hour
a mess of objects
surrounding tired feet

it wasn't hard
to find words
for once

in a whisper of fingers
like a gamma ray burst
along the spine
too fast
shot with nostalgia
gone before
dawn.

Out of the Blue

Here in the outer
solar system
it's colder, but there's a
certain, let's say
realism, that I
can take further

while you sit
in the humdrum glow of
all those safe, small
rocky spaces
fragile and fertile

you could have years
down there
missing me, feeling the
gutted sheen of
my absence in your
earthly heart

I'm icing over
lips blue like the
great dark spot of Neptune
crystals of frozen methane
raining down as diamonds

I'm not sure you'd
recognise me now
maybe by mathematical
prediction rather than
empirical observation
proof in the bones
in traces of carbon
in scent
rather than sight.

Intelligent Equations

It's not enough to wash the
stars throw shadows round
the room, ice particles
with your sweet soft touch in
the vacuum of light that hits
my solar plexus.

With any number of loose
technological
civilisations warming
things are bound

to get hot, better ice
the planet hug the low
lying islands close to our
chests every tear
another melting ice cap.

Reshaping the galaxy
in this way is not like
writing intelligent
equations for the rest of
our lives, holed up in pods
substituting ink with
type, all those elegant
letters and sensual
subscripts, like approximate
models of goodness
lost in time
waiting for an answer.

Notes

'Encroachment Spells Erosion' is a found poem. Every word has been found within the text of James Joyce's *Finnegan's Wake*.

'A Cloud Withdrew' is a redaction from Emily Dickinson's 'A Cloud Withdrew from the Sky' (895).

'Landscape at Pentecost' is an ekphrastic poem after *Landscape at Pentecost* by Grace Cossington Smith (circa 1932).

In 'Six Realms', 'the dull smoke coloured light/from hell' is from *The Tibetan Book of the Dead*.

'Inside Your Darkest Everything' is from a line in *The Diary of Frida Kahlo: An Intimate Self-Portrait*: 'I want to be inside your darkest everything.'

'Unceasing, unchanging murmur' is a line from 'Two Gallants' in *Dubliners* by James Joyce: 'Like illumined pearls the lamps shone from the summits of their tall poles upon the living texture below which, changing shape and hue unceasingly, sent up into the warm grey evening air, an unceasing, unchanging murmur.'

'Woman with her Hair Loose' is an ekphrastic poem after *Head of a Woman with Her Hair Loose* by Vincent van Gogh, December 1885, Antwerp.

'Gargantua Redacted' is a found poem taken from the text of *Gargantua and Pantagruel* by by François Rabelais.

Acknowledgements

Versions of these poems have been published in *Silver Birch Press, Tweetspeak Poetry, work & tumble 2015 Anthology, Tincture. Cordite, ARTS ZINE, Verity La, Bluepepper, Journal of Poetics Research, policies & procedures: poems by rob walker, Medical Journal of Australia, Best Australian Science Writing 2016, Indelible: 2015 PATP anthology*, and *The Fem*.

'Mapping Pluto' was shortlisted in 2015 Bayside Poetry Awards.

Versions of 'Watagan Walk' and 'Redhead Beach' were awarded commendations in the Morisset Show Lake Macquarie Moments competition.

'Nature's Conservatory' won second prize in Catchfire Press's Home is the Hunter competition and published in an anthology of the same name.

Versions of 'Alien World', 'Reflecting Sphere', 'Walking into Eternity', 'Coral Composition' and 'Landscape at Pentecost' appeared in the chapbook *Sublime Planet* by Magdalena Ball and Carolyn Howard-Johnson, 2014.

www.ingramcontent.com/pod-product-compliance
Lightning Source LLC
Chambersburg PA
CBHW071840080526
44589CB00012B/1064